Cornerstones of Freedom

The United States Holocaust Memorial Museum

Philip Brooks

CHILDREN'S PRESS®
A Division of Grolier Publishing
New York • London • Hong Kong • Sydney
Danbury, Connecticut

Library of Congress Cataloging-in-Publication Data

Brooks, Philip, 1963–
    The U.S. Holocaust Memorial Museum / by Philip Brooks.
        p. cm.—(Cornerstones of freedom)
    Includes index.
    Summary: Describes the planning and building of the U.S.
Holocaust Memorial Museum and examines its exhibits
documenting the European Holocaust from 1933 to 1945.
    ISBN 0-516-20007-0 (lib. bdg.) — ISBN 0-516-26071-5 (pbk.)
    1. U.S. Holocaust Memorial Museum—Exhibitions—Juvenile
literature. 2. Holocaust, Jewish (1939–1945)—Exhibitions—
Juvenile literature. [1. U.S. Holocaust Memorial Museum. 2.
Holocaust, Jewish (1939–1945) 3. Museums.] I. Title. II. Series.
D804.3.U2B76 1996
940.53′ 18—dc20
                                                    95-18633
                                                       CIP
                                                        AC

On April 26, 1993, the United States Holocaust Memorial Museum, located in Washington, D.C., opened its doors to the public. Inside, the story of one of the darkest chapters in human history is told. Between 1933 and 1945, the Nazi government of Germany murdered six million Jewish people throughout Europe. Millions of non-Jews were slaughtered, as well. Among the Nazis' victims were 1.5 million children.

The United States Holocaust Memorial Museum, in Washington, D.C.

Adolf Hitler

Why did the Nazis hate the Jews so much? Adolf Hitler became Germany's chancellor, the most powerful position in the German government, in 1933. During that time, Germany was suffering from major economic troubles. Many people were unemployed and hungry. Hitler delivered emotional speeches in which he blamed all of Germany's troubles on the Jews. He said that Germany's Jews had conspired to destroy the country for their own profit. He convinced many Germans to believe this lie, even though most Jews were loyal German patriots. Hundreds of Jews had fought and died for Germany in World War I (1914–1918).

Until the 1930s, the Jewish community in Germany had been highly successful. Jews had their own customs, neighborhoods, businesses, and places of worship. But they were considered "different." Germans found it easy to blame the Jews for the nation's hardships.

While Hitler's powerful armies conquered much of Europe early in World War II (which began in 1939), he and his advisors secretly engineered a plan to commit genocide—the intentional destruction of an entire ethnic group. They called this plan the "Final Solution to the Jewish Problem." The Nazis built concentration camps, which were factories for gathering people together and then murdering them. Only Nazi Germany's defeat by the Allies in 1945 ended the killing. By then, two out of every three Jews in Europe were dead. Whole families perished. The entire populations of villages vanished. A thousand years of Jewish culture were gone forever.

Millions of Europeans were murdered in Nazi concentration camps.

Nazis did not reserve their hatred only for Jews. Millions of others were considered enemies of Germany. Gypsies, Jehovah's Witnesses, homosexuals, communists, people with physical or mental disabilities, and anyone who had tried to help Jews escape death were exterminated in Hitler's Final Solution.

In the concentration camps, very few prisoners survived slave labor, brutal beatings, disease, terror, and starvation. It is almost impossible to

Starving prisoners were housed in overcrowded, filthy barracks.

imagine anyone living through such horror. But many of those who did survive say they wanted to live to stand as witnesses to what happened in the camps. They wanted to remember those who had been murdered and to make sure that such things never happened again.

Miles Lerman

In 1941, a young Jew named Miles Lerman was imprisoned in a slave labor camp near Lvov, Poland. In the camp, Lerman witnessed the Nazi guards force a Jewish father to choose which of his two sons would be hanged. The father closed his eyes and reached out to touch one of his sons at random. He was then forced to hang the boy. The father committed suicide the next morning. Miles Lerman escaped from the labor camp several months later. Haunted by what he had seen, he fought the German army alongside supporters of the Polish government. Lerman helped raid Nazi food warehouses, steal or destroy Nazi fuel supplies, and shoot at Nazi patrols. When the war ended, he learned that his entire family had been killed in a concentration camp called Belzec.

Lerman eventually moved to the United States, married another Holocaust survivor, and built a successful business in New Jersey. He and his wife did not try to forget all that they had seen and suffered. They believed it was their duty to teach others, especially young people, about the *Shoah,* or Holocaust.

At the end of World War II, Jewish immigrants from Europe resettled in Israel and the United States.

After World War II ended in 1945, many Holocaust memorials and museums were established throughout Europe and Israel. But Miles Lerman thought there should be a permanent national memorial in the United States, where so many survivors had resettled.

In 1980, President Jimmy Carter appointed Lerman to the United States Holocaust Memorial Council. The council was asked to design and build a national memorial to victims of the Nazis. Elie Wiesel, a Holocaust survivor who is well-known for the many books he has written about the Holocaust, was chairman of the council.

Elie Wiesel

The council, made up of people from various ethnic and religious backgrounds, disagreed on what, exactly, the museum should be. Some people argued that it should be a "Jewish museum" since Jews were the Nazis' main target for extermination. Other members insisted that murdered non-Jews deserved equal space in the new museum. Still others believed the museum should also memorialize those who had died in other genocidal events throughout history.

The council finally decided to build the museum in Washington, D.C., the nation's capital. The exhibits would teach visitors about the Holocaust in Europe from 1933 to 1945, and would concentrate on the Nazis' destruction of the Jews. The museum would also acknowledge and document all the other people who suffered at the hands of the Nazis. The council agreed that this would be the best way to honor both the survivors and the dead.

The United States government provided free land near the Washington Monument on which to build the museum. All funds for the building and exhibits were raised privately. Miles Lerman, Elie Wiesel, and many others worked hard to raise more than $200 million. In addition to raising money, museum organizers requested that people donate artifacts and documents for the museum's collection.

One of the most important donations came from the government of Poland. Many of the Nazi concentration camps were in Poland because Germany conquered it early in World War II. In 1987, Miles Lerman helped to negotiate an agreement with Poland's leaders to gain access to Nazi records and Holocaust artifacts that had never been seen by Western scholars. Lerman signed the agreement at Belzec, the concentration camp where his family had perished.

Museum planners faced a difficult problem in searching for a design for the museum building. They wondered what type of building design and exhibits they could choose that would best express the unspeakable horrors of the Holocaust. This could not be a museum like any other museum. The planners wanted a visitor's experience to be a sad one, but they also wanted visitors to feel a sense of hope and a determination to end hate in the world.

James Ingo Freed and his sister escaped the Holocaust; but these Jewish children were not as lucky. German troops are rounding them up for removal to a concentration camp.

In 1986, the task of designing the United States Holocaust Memorial Museum was given to James Ingo Freed, an architect with the firm of Pei, Cobb, Freed and Partners in New York City. Freed was Jewish, and was born in Essen, Germany, but he and his family escaped the Holocaust. His parents sent him and his sister to the United States in 1939, when he was nine years old. His parents joined them in 1941.

When the project was assigned to him, Freed had no idea what sort of building he would design. He began to study the Holocaust. He read many books and watched every documentary film available. The more he learned, the more difficult his responsibility seemed.

For a long time, Freed thought the job would be impossible to complete. Then Freed traveled to Germany and toured Auschwitz and other

Nazi death camps. When he saw the camps, Freed sensed that isolation and sorrow still hung in the air. But while he was there, he began to envision what the Holocaust Memorial Museum should look like. He decided that the barbed-wire fences, ugly brick buildings, and imposing guard towers

Nazi guards watched camp prisoners from guard towers (above). Auschwitz is infamous for the number of deaths that took place there (right).

would be part of his design. But he knew that just reconstructing a concentration camp would not work. Instead of reproducing the camps, Freed decided to make "visual references" to them throughout the museum.

The front of the Holocaust Museum building is made of limestone, just like many of the monuments and museums in Washington, D.C. But here, the limestone front is not the real entrance to the building. The doors are found further inside. The real entrance is hidden, to symbolize the way the Nazis tried to hide what was happening in the concentration camps from the rest of the world.

The actual doors to the Holocaust Museum are almost completely hidden from view.

The Hall of Witness

Once inside, visitors enter the Hall of Witness. Brick walls rise high. At the ceiling, the walls meet heavy steel beams that block the light from the skylights above. Everywhere there are brick walls, bare steel beams, and gray concrete. The floor of the hall is deliberately cracked to symbolize the way civilization broke down during the years of the Holocaust. A gray steel staircase at the end of the hall becomes narrower toward the top and ends with a brick arch. This reminds visitors of the train tracks that led to the arched gate of the Birkenau death camp.

Glass-and-steel walkways symbolize the constant scrutiny that prisoners endured.

At several points in the museum, exposed walkways loom above visitors. These glass-and-steel walkways echo with the footsteps of other visitors. In the real camps, the footsteps were made by the boots of Nazi guards armed with machine guns. Through the museum's windows and skylights, visitors can see brick pyramids on the roof similar to guard towers.

The museum's permanent exhibition begins on the fourth floor and spirals downward to the third, second, and first floors. Before beginning this journey, each visitor is given an identity card. The card shows the photo of a person who lived in Europe during the Holocaust and carries a brief summary of that person's life. Some of the people on these cards survived, others did not. Computer stations in the museum provide information about the fate of the person on the identity card. The purpose of the cards is to make each visitor's experience at the museum a very personal one.

Visitors to the museum can choose identity cards that match their age and gender.

To begin viewing the exhibit, visitors ride an elevator to the fourth floor. The elevator is lit by bulbs in metal cages. The walls are covered in dull, gray steel. The doors clank shut to create the feeling that the bright, modern world of Washington, D.C., has been left behind and a cold, dark world has been entered.

The fourth floor of the museum depicts the rapid rise of Nazism in Germany in the 1930s. Texts, artifacts, photographs, and videotapes reveal Hitler's rise from a minor figure in German politics, to the chancellorship, without the Nazi Party ever winning a popular election. Once in power, Hitler quickly began to persecute Jews. On April 1, 1933, the Nazis established a boycott of all Jewish businesses and shops

The Nazis instituted a boycott of all Jewish businesses and shops in Germany.

Nazi propaganda is displayed at the Holocaust Museum.

throughout Germany. Race laws that isolated Jews and took away many of their rights were passed soon after.

The Nazis then began firing Jewish professors and burning books written by Jews. Nazi propaganda convinced the German people that the Jews were destroying German society. Propaganda is written material, speeches, posters, or films created with the intention of doing damage to other people. Most propaganda is false. Hitler and his chief propagandist, Joseph Goebbels, turned public opinion against the Jews. Many examples of Nazi propaganda are on display at the museum.

On November 9, 1938, a wave of anti-Jewish violence swept across Germany. Nazi soldiers and German citizens looted and destroyed about seven thousand Jewish businesses. Centuries-old synagogues were set afire. Jewish cemeteries were vandalized. Ninety-six Jews were reported murdered. So many windows were smashed that November 9 has come to be known as *Kristallnacht,* or "the Night of Broken Glass." The Holocaust Memorial Museum contains photographs of that terrible night. Other evidence on display includes burned prayer books and a piece of a destroyed synagogue's doorway. A hate message from the Nazis is scrawled on the door.

Seven thousand Jewish businesses were damaged or destroyed on the night of November 9, 1938.

The fourth floor exhibit concludes with Hitler's invasion and conquest of Poland on September 1, 1939. Photographs and texts reveal that the Polish Jews quickly became victims of the Nazi reign of terror. The same month that the Nazis marched through Poland, Hitler signed an order stating that any people considered "unfit to live" (mainly, old people and people with physical limitations) would be killed. The Nazis described these murders as "mercy killings." A hospital bed with restraint straps that the Nazis used for these murders is on display.

The third floor begins by describing with words and photographs the isolation of Jews within walled ghettos throughout Nazi-occupied Europe. These ghettos were overcrowded, filthy places without enough food to support the population. Artifacts include examples of the yellow cloth Star of David that all Jews in areas under Nazi control were forced to sew onto their clothing. A two-wheeled handcart on display was used to transport heavy loads, often the bodies of those who died of starvation.

German law required Jews to wear yellow Stars of David with the word, "Jude" (Jew), sewn onto their clothing.

There is an exhibit about Anne Frank, the young girl who is famous for the diary she kept while hiding from the Nazis in Amsterdam, the Netherlands. Exhibits also reveal the efforts people made to document the crimes of the Nazis. There is a model built by Leon Jacobson that depicts in exact detail the Jewish ghetto in Lodz, Poland. To keep the model hidden, Jacobson wrapped it in paper and buried it in the basement of his building. It was found at the end of the war.

The next display at the museum reveals the horrors of the Nazi concentration camps to

Anne Frank

Concentration camps were enclosed with barbed wire to prevent prisoners from escaping.

visitors. In the spring of 1945, the war in Europe was rapidly ending as German troops retreated. American, British, and Soviet troops (the Allies) liberated one region after another from Nazi rule. As the Allies freed these places, they discovered barbed wire-enclosed concentration camps. The names of a few of these camps were Auschwitz, Birkenau, Treblinka, Chelmno, and Sobibor. Under orders defined by the Final Solution, Jews and others considered to be "undesirables" had been forced from their homes and transported by train to these places for extermination.

Inside the camps, Allied soldiers encountered unimaginable horrors. Journalist H. W. Lawrence, after seeing a camp called Majdenek, wrote: "I have just seen the most terrible place on earth." Prisoners who had managed to survive looked like living skeletons. Their eyes were hollow and they were either naked or clothed only in rags. Their skin was covered with sores, filth, and lice. Their heads were shaved, and blue identification numbers had been tattooed on their arms. Even several weeks after they were freed, many of these victims died of starvation, disease, and exhaustion.

Everywhere horrified soldiers looked, they found naked, emaciated corpses. In some camps,

Few prisoners survived long enough to be liberated by the Allies.

the corpses were stacked twenty high. Thousands of others had been dumped and buried in shallow mass graves by fleeing Nazi guards.

Even veteran soldiers who had seen the worst of war could not believe their eyes. General Dwight D. Eisenhower, the supreme commander of the Allied forces, toured a camp in Germany called

General Dwight D. Eisenhower (center) witnessed the horrors of this Nazi concentration camp.

Ohrdruf. He insisted on seeing every inch of the camp. He felt it was his duty "to be in a position from then on to testify at first hand about these things in case there ever grew up at home [the United States] the belief . . . that the stories about Nazi brutality were just propaganda."

But overwhelming evidence proves that the Holocaust was real. In the museum, video monitors show films of some of the horrors of the death camps. These films depict the cruel medical experiments performed on men, women, and children. Exhibited is a casting of a door from one of the gas chambers used to murder hundreds of people at the same time. Visitors can walk through a railroad boxcar that was used to transport victims to the concentration camps.

A detailed plaster model of a crematorium recreates one of the killing stations found in Auschwitz. Here, victims arrived by train and were then inspected by camp guards. Those considered unable to work were "selected"— meaning, killed immediately. The victims (mostly, women and children) were led down a set of stairs to a dressing room. Guards told them they would be taking a shower. They were forced to give up all of their valuables and to take off their clothes. Then they were led into a room with shower heads. The air-tight doors were locked, the lights went off, and a poisonous gas called Zyklon-B was released into the chamber, killing everyone inside. Other prisoners were forced to carry out the dead bodies. These prisoners were ordered to remove any gold teeth they found in the mouths of the dead, and shave the hair from the heads of the dead women. The bodies were then burned in specially designed ovens.

Women and children were often selected for gassing immediately following their arrival in the camps (below). Empty containers of Zyklon-B (below, right)

Prisoners cheer the arrival of the Allies to their concentration camp—April 30, 1945.

The second floor details the liberation of the camps and the world's response to what was found in them. Film clips show the trials of Nazi war criminals, which were held in Nuremberg, Germany, in 1946. Many of the Nazi leaders were hanged for their crimes. Others spent the rest of their lives in prison. Adolf Hitler could not be tried because he committed suicide in 1945, just prior to the end of the war.

Photographs of Holocaust victims line the walls of the museum.

Photographs detail the mass emigration of Holocaust survivors to Israel and the United States in the years after the war. Finally, a small theater shows continuous films of survivors telling their stories. These peoples' experiences—the murders of parents, children, relatives, and friends—are very sad. But these eyewitnesses tell their stories so that their accounts can never be forgotten.

Also on the second floor, a special exhibit documents the heroic acts of Jews and non-Jews in the face of Nazi terror. Many people in countries occupied by the Nazis hid Jews in their homes. Brave local officials sometimes falsified records so that Nazi soldiers could not deport Jews from their communities. The names of these heroes, and their deeds, are recorded on a white wall. This wall celebrates incredible compassion in the face of a brutal enemy.

An exhibit for children called "Daniel's Story" is on the first floor. It uses videotape, full-sized settings, and a fictional diary to tell the story of a Jewish boy who is taken from his home and forced to live in the ghetto in Lodz. He and his family are then deported to the Auschwitz concentration camp.

The Hall of Remembrance symbolizes the sadness—and hope—of the Holocaust Memorial Museum.

A visitor's journey through the museum ends at the Hall of Remembrance. This is a beautiful, six-sided room filled with light from skylights and hidden openings in the walls. A flame burns above a stone box that contains earth taken from the actual camps where so many people perished. The room is a place where designer James Ingo Freed hoped visitors would feel deep sadness for those who died, but also great joy for those who lived.

In the museum's Wexner Learning Center, interactive computers allow visitors to view films, photographs, and maps. This technology helps visitors learn more about specific events, places, or people involved with the Holocaust that interest them.

The museum library, called the Hall of Learning, contains Holocaust books and documents gathered from all over the world. The nearby Registry of Jewish Holocaust Survivors collects information on survivors, including their oral histories and photographs. Together, the library and registry comprise the United States Holocaust Museum Research Institute. The institute enables the museum to serve as an international center for Holocaust research. Two auditoriums are available for films, lectures, and conventions.

On the lower level of the museum, the Children's Wall of Remembrance is made up of more than three thousand ceramic tiles. Each was painted by an American schoolchild to express his or her feelings about the Holocaust. The wall is the museum's tribute to the 1.5 million children murdered by the Nazis. Also, the Gonda Education Center offers classrooms for school groups that visit the museum, and a Teacher's Resource Center to help teachers discuss the Holocaust with their students.

Schoolchildren painted ceramic tiles for the Children's Wall of Remembrance.

The United States Holocaust Memorial Museum is located near the Washington Monument, the Smithsonian Institution, and the United States Capitol. The official dedication took place on April 22, 1993, a cold and rainy Thursday. President Bill Clinton said, "This is a place of deep sadness, but it will also become a sanctuary of bright hope. Here on the town square of our national life . . . we dedicate the United States Holocaust Memorial Museum, and so bind one of the darkest lessons of history to the hopeful soul of America."

The official dedication of the Holocaust Memorial Museum was held on April 22, 1993.

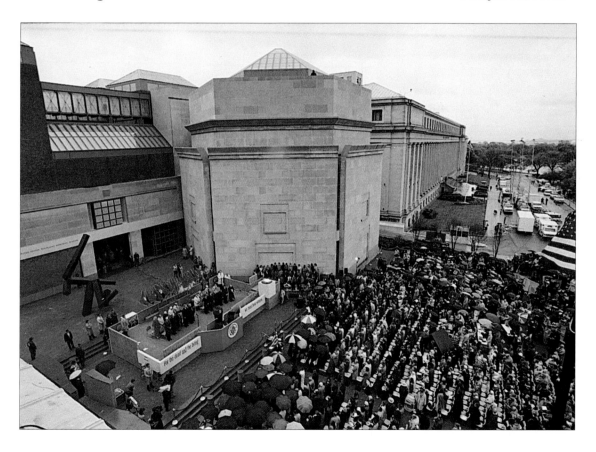

GLOSSARY

Allies – countries united against Germany in World War II; the Allies included the United States, England, and the Soviet Union

architect – person who designs buildings and oversees their construction

artifact – object from a specific period in history

civilization – society that is culturally and technologically advanced

concentration camp

concentration camp – guarded prison where Jews and others were imprisoned and murdered by Nazis during World War II

crematorium – building where dead bodies were burned

dictator – person who controls a country without ever being elected by the country's citizens

dictator

ghetto – section of a city in which people live in poverty

holocaust – mass destruction; the Nazi plan of genocide is called "The Holocaust"

imposing – very large or impressive in size

liberate – to free from another group's control

synagogue – place where Jewish people worship

TIMELINE

Germans defend yourselves against jewish atrocity propaganda buy only at German shops!

Hitler becomes chancellor; Nazi boycott of Jewish businesses begins

November 9: Kristallnacht ("Night of Broken Glass")

"Final Solution" devised

War ends; concentration camps liberated

United States Holocaust Memorial Council established

1933

1935 Jews stripped of German citizenship

1938

1939 World War II begins in Europe

1940 Jews forced into ghettos; Auschwitz opened

1941

1942

1945

1948 Israel founded

1980

1993 *April 22:* United States Holocaust Memorial Museum dedicated

September 1: Jews forced to wear yellow Stars of David

INDEX (*Boldface page numbers indicate illustrations.*)

PHOTO CREDITS

©: John Skowronski/Folio, Inc.: Cover, pp. 13, 14 (bottom), 27; AP/Wide World: pp. 1, 7, 18, 20 (top), 29, 31 (right, both photos); Archive Photos: pp. 4, 11, 16, 20 (bottom), 22, 30 (bottom), 31 (top left); G. D. Hackett/Archive Photos: p. 24 (left); Bettmann Archive: pp. 25, 31 (bottom left); AFP/Bettmann: p. 3; UPI/Bettmann: pp. 6, 8, 9, 23, 30 (top); Cameramann International, Ltd: p. 12 (top); Folio, Inc.: pp. 14 (top), 26; Gorani, Inc./Folio, Inc.: pp. 15, 19, 28; Phoebe Bell/Folio, Inc.: pp. 2, 17; Andrew Lichtenstein/Impact Visuals: p. 24 (right); Sean Sprague/Impact Visuals: pp. 5, 12 (bottom); Photri, Inc.: p. 21

ABOUT THE AUTHOR

Philip Brooks grew up near Chicago and now lives in Ohio, with his wife, Balinda Craig-Quijada. He attended the University of Iowa Writers' Workshop, where he received an M.F.A. in fiction writing. His stories have appeared in a number of literary magazines, and he has written several books for children. He is the author of *Michael Jordan: Beyond Air* and *Dikembe Mutombo* for Children's Press, and the Franklin Watts First Books *Georgia O'Keeffe* and *Mary Cassatt*.